The Other Side

Copyright © 1979, Grisewood and Dempsey

Library of Congress Number: 78-21018

1 2 3 4 5 6 7 8 9 0 83 82 81 80 79

Printed in the United States of America.

Library of Congress Cataloging in Publication Data

Manley, Deborah.
  The other side.

  SUMMARY: Text and pictures introduce opposites
such as full and empty, clean and dirty, and short
and long.
  1. English language — Synonyms and antonyms —
Juvenile literature. [1. English language —
Synonyms and antonyms] I. Astrop, John.
II. Title.
PE1591.M35 428'.1 78-21018
ISBN 0-8172-1301-5 lib. bdg.

The Other Side

Words by
Deborah Manley

Pictures by
John Astrop

RAINTREE CHILDRENS BOOKS
Milwaukee • Toronto • Melbourne • London

The children are on their way to the circus. They are having a hard time getting the donkey to move. The donkey is very slow.

It will not take these children long to get to the circus. The horse they are riding is very fast. Name some other animals that are fast. What animals are slow?

On the way to the circus, the children see some pigs. Some of the pigs are clean.

Some of the pigs are dirty. How many dirty pigs are there?

The children see a pen full of sheep. How many sheep are in the pen?

This pen is empty!

Full and *empty* are opposites. So are *clean* and *dirty*. Opposites come in pairs. One word means something completely different from the other.

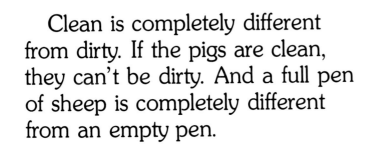

Clean is completely different from dirty. If the pigs are clean, they can't be dirty. And a full pen of sheep is completely different from an empty pen.

11

The children see some clowns at the circus. How many clowns are there? What are the clowns doing?

Which clowns are thin? Which clowns are fat?

Can the thin clown also be a fat clown?

Here are more clowns. The thin
clown is at the top of the ladder.
Where is the fat clown?
What are the two pairs of
opposites in this picture?

What is wrong with the way the clown is sitting on the donkey? What do you think will happen to the clown when the donkey begins to move? Which way do you think the clown will go? Which way will the donkey go?

These clowns are happy. They are all smiling. How many happy clowns are there?

These clowns are sad. How can
you tell that they are not happy?

The elephant and its friends are playing.

The elephant is very big. Can
you name the animals that
are small?

The giraffe is very tall.

So is the bird. Which animals
are short?

Which way are the clown and
the animals facing? Can you see
the front of the clown?

Which part of the clown do you
see now?

The circus is moving. The clown is in the first car of the long train. How many cars are there? What are the colors of the last car?

The short train is riding over a long bridge. Can you find any short bridges? How many pairs of opposites can you find?

Look around you.

28

What opposites do you see?

This will help you with the Word Review.

a	**a** as in **cat**
ā	**a** as in **able**
ä	**a** as in **father**
e	**e** as in **bend**
ē	**e** as in **me**
i	**i** as in **in**
ī	**i** as in **ice**
o	**o** as in **top**
ō	**o** as in **old**
ô	**o** as in **cloth**
oo	**oo** as in **good**
o͞o	**oo** as in **tool**
oi	**oi** as in **oil**
ou	**ou** as in **out**
u	**u** as in **up**
ur	**ur** as in **fur**
yo͞o	**u** as in **use**
ə	**a** as in **again**
ch	**ch** as in **such**
ng	**ng** as in **sing**
sh	**sh** as in **shell**
th	**th** as in **three**
th̲	**th** as in **that**

Word Review

Here are some words from *The Other Side*. Practice saying each word out loud. See if you can find them in the book.

bridge (brij)
circus (sur′ kəs)
clean (klēn)
clown (kloun)
dirty (dur′ tē)
donkey (dong′ kē)
empty (emp′ tē)
fat (fat)
full (fool)
giraffe (jə raf′)
horse (hôrs)
ladder (lad′ ər)
opposite (op′ ə zit)
pair (per)
thin (thin)